Learning Strategy in a fun way with
THE BIG BANG THEORY

Rajesh K Pillania, Ph.D (Strategy)

Other Humorous Books by the Same Author

Strategic Humour: Democratizing Strategy

Love Strategy: A New Perspective on Love, Relationships, Life and Strategy.

Startup Humor: Democratizing Startup Strategy

Happiness Strategy: Strategy and Happiness for Everyone

*This book is dedicated to
all those who are interested in the challenging
but fascinating subject of "strategy"*

Book with a Social Cause

All royalties earned from this book will be donated to the cause of education.

Copyright

Copyright © Rajesh K Pillania

All rights reserved. No part of this publication may be reproduced, distributed or transmitted in any form or by any means, including photocopying, recording, or other electronic or mechanical methods, without the prior written permission of the author/ publisher, except in the case of brief quotations embodied in reviews and certain other non-commercial uses permitted by copyright laws.

Disclaimer

This book is a work of fiction and any resemblance with any individual, organization, situation, event, or work is a mere coincidence and the author bears no responsibility for the same.

For educational purpose it uses incidents from the popular American TV show The Big Bang Theory. We acknowledge this.

This book is written in a lighter vein and it doesn't intend to hurt anyone's sentiments or emotions.

Acknowledgment

This book wouldn't have been possible without support from number of people.

First of all, I acknowledge the very popular American TV show The Big Bang Theory. This book uses incidents from the show to explain strategy concepts.

I acknowledge the inputs received from my students and friends who are regular viewers of the show.

I acknowledge the critical inputs and proofreading the manuscript by Ms. Dearbhla O'Reilly.

Last, but not the least, I also acknowledge the strategy professors who have coined these strategy concepts over the years.

Preface

Learning needs to be fun!
It should be memorable.
It must be applied.

The above three principles are the reason behind this book. This book tries to explain forty strategy concepts in a fun and memorable way while engaging the reader to apply these concepts. To get the maximum benefit from this book, engagement of the reader is a must, and he/she needs to apply the concepts explained because ideas for sake of ideas doesn't take one anywhere.

This book explains strategy concepts by using incidents from the very popular American TV show The Big Bang Theory (TBBT). The book follows a simple modular approach. It can be read from any page. Every concept gets covered in two pages (excluding a few). Have fun!

Table of Content

Acknowledgment ix
Preface.. xi
An Unusual Meeting xv

1. Vision 1
2. Mission 3
3. Core Values 5
4. External Environment (PEST) Analysis 7
5. Industry Analysis 9
6. Internal Environment Analysis 11
7. Core Competence 13
8. SWOT analysis 15
9. Competitive Advantage 17
10. Value Addition 19
11. Value Chain Analysis... 21
12. Strategic Alternatives and Choice 23
13. Strategy 25
14. Tactics 27
15. Cost Leadership Strategy 29
16. Differentiation Strategy 31
17. Plan B 33
18. Scenario Planning 35
19. Diversification (Ansoff Matrix) 37
20. Strategic Alliances.. 39

21.	Co-opetition	41
22.	Business Model	43
23.	Strategy Execution	47
24.	Resource Allocation	49
25.	Growth Trap	51
26.	Focus & Discipline	53
27.	Curse of Knowledge	55
28.	Importance of Assumptions	57
29.	Paralysis by Analysis	59
30.	Strategic Alignment	61
31.	Entrepreneurship	63
32.	Innovation	65
33.	International Strategy	67
34.	Corporate Governance	69
35.	Strategic Corporate Social Responsibility (CSR)	71
36.	Organizational Structure	73
37.	McKinsey 7S Framework	75
38.	Emergent Strategy	77
39.	Balanced Scorecard	79
40.	Limitations of Strategy	81

The Landing Announcement	83
References	85
Appendix 1. Free Resources for Strategy	87
Brief Profile of the Author	89

AN UNUSUAL MEETING

On a direct flight from New Delhi to Chicago, people have started taking their seats on the plane.

Professor Husmukh Doordarshi has taken a window seat and there are two young men named Kapil and Pushkar in the two seats to his right. He is replying to some last minute phone calls before the flight takes off.

He overhears the casual talk between the two young men sitting next to him. They are going to an executive program in strategy and are not happy about the learnings from one such previous program. Professor Husmukh intervenes and they start a conversation.

Professor Husmukh: Sorry to intervene, but would you please share why you were not happy with one of the previous strategy program you attended.

Kapil: It all went above my head. It was all about how strategy was made by top management and its benefits and blah blah. I am at the beginning of my career and it appears strategy is mainly for top management. It is not relevant or applicable for me.

Pushkar: Plus, it was so dry and boring and with so much heavy jargon.

Professor Husmukh: Oh, sorry to hear that but strategy is not like that.

Incidentally Kapil is watching the Big Bang Theory (TBBT). The Professor asks if they are into this TV Series. They tell him they are huge fans of the Big Bang Theory. In fact, they have seen all the seasons and episodes and have videos of them on their laptops.

Professor: Great! I have an interesting idea. I will share an interesting incident from one of the episodes of the Big Bang Theory and give you one important strategy learning from that. If you don't like it, tell me and we stop. Otherwise we continue.

Kapil & Pushkar: That's great! We are game for it!

1. VISION

Let us start with Vision.

Here is a hilarious video for you from The Big Bang Theory (TBBT), season 6, episode 14.

The scene is Sheldon's office. Sheldon is solving a complex equation while imagining the response of an imaginary crowd. He is able to solve the equation and the imaginary crowd shouts 'Nobel! Nobel!' for him.

Ha ha! It is so funny!
In this video, Sheldon is imaging his future.
Sheldon's vision is to win a Nobel Prize for Physics.

Vision is what an organization aspires to be in the future. It should be a guiding and motivating force that is neither impossible to achieve nor easily attainable. It should be clear, brief and memorable.

Questions for you:

1. What is vision of your organisation?

   ....
   ....
   ....

2. Is it the right one? If yes, why?

   ....
   ....
   ....

3. If it is not the right one, what it should be?

   ....
   ....
   ....

2. MISSION

Here you go with another fun video from TBBT, session 8, episode 17.

In one scene, Sheldon and Amy are in the Apartment. Sheldon has applied to go to Mars. He has made a video as a part of his application. He shares the video with Amy. In this video, Sheldon is extolling his virtues in a funny way. He then says on a serious note that the most important reason for him to go to Mars is that as a scientist it is his responsibility to push forward the boundaries of human knowledge.

Ha ha ha! It is so hilarious!

On a serious note, the video shows that Sheldon cares about the future of mankind. Though he wants to win a Nobel prize for Physics, he also wants to contribute to the future of mankind using his mental faculties to come up with new theories.

Mission means the core purpose of an organization. It justifies the organization's existence. It should be clear, brief and memorable.

Questions for you:

1. What is mission of your organisation?

   ....
   ....
   ....

2. Is it the right one? If yes, why?

   ....
   ....
   ....

3. If it is not the right one, what it should be?

   ....
   ....
   ....

3. CORE VALUES

Let's watch this fun video from TBBT, series 6, episode 7.

As you have seen, at one point in this episode, Sheldon gets drunk and he is at Wil Wheaton's house. He goes there to fight with Wil Wheaton because Wil Wheaton has insulted his girlfriend Amy. Sheldon feels honour bound to defend her. Wil Wheaton says sorry for his behavior and then Sheldon proceeds to throw up outside Wil's house as he is drunk.

Ha ha ha! It is so hilarious!

On a serious note, the video shows that Sheldon's core values tell him to protect Amy, his girlfriend.

He goes to Wil Wheaton to challenge him and seek an apology from him as he feels Will has disrespected Amy.

Core values are the core principles of the organization which are deep rooted in the organization, define its culture, bind its people together and cannot be compromised for short term benefits or convenience.

Questions for you:

1. What are the core values of your organization?

   ....
   ....
   ....

2. Are these the right ones? If yes, why?

   ....
   ....
   ....

3. If these are not the right ones, what these should be?

   ....
   ....
   ....

4. EXTERNAL ENVIRONMENT (PEST) ANALYSIS

Let us watch another gem from TBBT, series 11, episode 22.

As you have seen, at one point in this episode, Sheldon goes to a Casino in Las Vegas. Based on his suspicious behavior he is intercepted by the security. He tells the security that he is a physicist and has been observing the wheel for hours and has run a chi-square analysis to find out the ball is likely to land on 32, 17 or 5. He wants to place a bet and claims he is doing this to earn money for science but he is taken out of the Casino by security.

Ha Ha! It is real entertainment! Sheldon is trying to make some money in a Casino in Las Vegas.

From the political environment aspect, the administration in Las Vegas allows gambling. From the economic environment aspect, there is enough money with people gambling in Las Vegas. Sheldon also has money. From the social environment aspect, it is socially acceptable to gamble in Las Vegas. From the technology environment aspect, technology is not very advanced in Roulette. Sheldon is able to figure out his chances of winning using math.

The external environment (PEST) analysis looks good to Sheldon for gambling in Las Vegas and he goes there to make some money for science.

The external environment is the macro environment in which an organization exists. One tool to analyse this environment is the PEST (political, economic, social and technological) analysis.

Questions for you:

1. How is external environment analysis for your organization?

   ....
   ....
   ....

2. Is it favourable? If yes, why?

   ....
   ....
   ....

3. If it is not favourable, how are you going to take care of it?

   ....
   ....
   ....

5. INDUSTRY ANALYSIS

Here is a hilarious video from TBBT for you, season 4, episode 12.

In this scene, the friends are in the University cafeteria. There, Leonard shares his idea of developing an app to solve differential equations. His idea is to build an app that uses handwriting recognition and then runs it through a symbolic evaluation engine to solve equations. One needs to just take a picture using a smartphone and run it through the app to solve it.

Ha Ha! I love this show! In this video, Leonard has an idea for an app for solving differential equations. We can look at the industry analysis for this app.

Competitive Rivalry: Since there is no other application which solves differential equations by just clicking a picture, there is no competition in the market.

Bargaining Power of Buyer: There are no alternatives for the application in the market. Therefore, buyer power is weak.

Bargaining Power of Supplier: They themselves are the main suppliers for creating this app as the main input in this app is the knowledge for creating this app, which they themselves have.

Threat of New Entrants: The development of the application requires advanced scientific and mathematical knowledge. This limits the entry into the market since few people would be able to develop such an application.

Threat of Substitutes: Right now, the only substitute is doing it manually which is not convenient. In future other apps may come.

This is a profitable industry to enter for them.

For industry analysis, the Five Force analysis tool is used. The collective strength of these five forces determines the ultimate profit potential or attractiveness of an industry.

Questions for you:

1. How is industry analysis for your organization?

   ....
   ....
   ....

2. Is it profitable? If yes, why?

   ....
   ....
   ....

3. If it is not profitable, how are you going to take care of it?

   ....
   ....
   ....

6. INTERNAL ENVIRONMENT ANALYSIS

Let me share another funny video from TBBT, season 8, episode 2.

The scene is Leonard and Sheldon's apartment. Leonard, Sheldon, Raj, and Howard are playing a game. The questions are difficult and they are praising themselves for knowing all the answers. Then Raj asks, why didn't girls like them in high school. Howard answers it by saying that they were awkward, weird and couldn't play sports. This answer is supported by Leonard. And they keep playing the game.

It is so funny! Ha ha!

In this episode Sheldon and his friends are playing a game and are having a blast. They feel they are very smart. Then suddenly one of them ask why girls didn't like them in high school. Another one states their weaknesses of being weird, awkward and didn't play sports. This is a fun way of carrying out internal analysis.

The self-analysis of finding internal strengths and weaknesses of an organization is called internal environment analysis.

Questions for you:

1. How is the internal environment analysis for your organization?

   ....
   ....
   ....

2. Is it favourable? If yes, why?

   ....
   ....
   ....

3. If it is not favourable, how are you going to take care of it?

   ....
   ....
   ....

7. CORE COMPETENCE

Let us watch this hilarious video from your favourite TBBT, season 10, episode 13.

In this episode, Sheldon and Amy are in the spa and they are joined there by Penny and Leonard. Sheldon asks them are they still fighting and are they going to get divorced. He wants to know if he will get two Christmases. Penny tells Sheldon they are not getting divorced and Leonard requests Sheldon to help them by writing a relationship agreement for them. Sheldon gets excited by this and agrees to start working on it ASAP. Amy laughs hearing this from Sheldon and says she has to laugh because it is the part of their relationship agreement.

In this video, Leonard and Penny are facing some issues in their marriage and they realise one way to solve the issues can be a relationship agreement to make things clear. They seek the help of Sheldon who is really good at making these agreements and enjoys giving advice. He is excited by their request. He prepares a detailed agreement with all the finer details of the complexities of their relationship. This is signed by both Leonard and Penny.

Making relationship agreements is one of the core competencies of Sheldon!

Core Competencies of an organization are the collective learnings which differentiate one organization from another and are difficult to copy by others.

Questions for you:

1. What are the core competencies of your organization?

   ....
   ....
   ....

2. Are they good enough? If yes, why?

   ....
   ....
   ....

3. If not, how are you going to take care of it?

   ....
   ....
   ....

8. SWOT ANALYSIS

Here is another hilarious one from TBBT, season 6, episode 2.

In the scene from this episode, Sheldon is standing next to Penny's bed in the middle of the night and wakes her up. She gets up slightly frightened and wonders why he is there. Sheldon asks her not to dump his friend Leonard as her boyfriend. He goes on to list all of the positive traits of Leonard, including the fact he is an attractive and desirable boyfriend as he has a perfect driving record and enjoys the insurance discounts because of that, how while he may not be tall in the US, he is definitely considered average height in North Korea and so on.

Ha ha! It is so funny! In the video, there is this hilarious scene when Sheldon goes to Penny in the middle of the night when she is sleeping. He goes because he came to know from Amy that Penny may end her relationship with Leonard. There, Sheldon tries to convince Penny to not end the relationship and to avoid hurting his friend. The scene is hilarious. From that scene, we can infer, Sheldon has done a SWOT Analysis of Leonard as a boyfriend for Penny.

Strengths: Perfect driving record, Has Insurance, Likes Penny, is Sheldon's friend.

Weaknesses: Not tall (but average if compared to North Korean)

Opportunities: Trying out other men.

Threats: Of losing friendship with Sheldon and the gang.

Strength, Weakness, Opportunities and Threat or SWOT analysis looks in totality at both external as well as internal environment of an organization.

Questions for you:

1. How is SWOT analysis for your organization?

   ....
   ....
   ....

2. Is it favourable? If yes, why?

   ....
   ....
   ....

3. If not, how are you going to take care of it?

   ....
   ....
   ....

9. COMPETITIVE ADVANTAGE

Let me share another fun video from TBBT, season 6, episode 4.

As you have seen, at one point in this episode, in the apartment, Penny and Amy are playing Pictionary Vs. Sheldon and Leonard. The boys lose all three rounds. All three rounds are simple words. In the first round, Sheldon cannot get Leonard to guess even after taking a long time to draw their word. Sheldon gets the third word wrong and can't even illustrate that! Penny doesn't even start drawing the third word for a long time, watching amusingly the funny pictures made by Sheldon and the awkward guesses made by Leonard.

Ha ha! It is so much fun watching this video!

In this video they are playing Pictionary game in two teams of Penny and Amy Vs Sheldon and Leonard. Penny is street smart and that is her competitive advantage. She explains the words simply.

Competitive advantage refers to how one company is better than others in a given industry. Competitive advantage is creating a wider gap than your competition between the maximum price a buyer is willing to pay and the lowest price below which the supplier will not sell.

Questions for you:

1. What is competitive advantage of your organization?

   ....
   ....
   ....

2. Is it sustainable? If yes, why?

   ....
   ....
   ....

3. If not, how are you going to take care of it?

   ....
   ....
   ....

10. VALUE ADDITION

Let me show you a small video clip from the TBBT season 4, episode 19.

In this episode, Sheldon has been the victim of online fraud. Someone hacked his World of Warcraft account and stole his loot. The three friends go with Sheldon to take back his stuff from Todd Zarneki but he takes more stuff from Sheldon! Penny comes to pick them up in her car and asks them about their stuff. Learning that Todd Zarneki was mean to them, she goes back to his house with them and asks for his stuff. Todd refuses to return the items and Penny hits him in the groin. Todd gives back the stuff and the boys come back happily from their quest to get back his stolen material!

This is hilarious!

In this video when Sheldon and his friends are unable to retrieve their belongings from the hacker they approach Penny. Penny with her courage and street smarts adds value to this group and helps Sheldon get back his belongings from the hacker. In this way, Penny adds value to the group in this situation.

Value addition means what value is added by an activity or an outside organization to an organization.

Questions for you:

1. What is value addition by your organization?

   ....
   ....
   ....

2. Is it good enough? If yes, why?

   ....
   ....
   ....

3. If not, how are you going to take care of it?

   ....
   ....
   ....

11. VALUE CHAIN ANALYSIS

Let me show you a small video clip from the TBBT, season 8, episode 2.

In this episode, Sheldon is in the office of Mrs. Davis. She suggests to Sheldon a solution solve his problem of changing his field of study. He is currently paid under a grant to research string theory. She suggests they could promote him to the junior professor and then he can change his field of research to a field of his choice. Sheldon thinks she is crazy for suggesting this solution in which he has to babysit a bunch of average graduate students who have little knowledge of physics.

This is hilarious. Here is the value chain for Sheldon as a scientist.

Secondary Activities	Technology Scientific equipment, laptops, emails, mobile.				
	Human Resource Management His assistant, co-authors, friends.				
	Procurement Scientific books, papers and attending conferences.				
	Firm Infrastructure Laboratory				
Primary Activities	Inbound Logistics	Operations	Outbound Logistics	Marketing & Sales	Service
	Scientific research material and knowledge	Reading and thought experiments	Research papers and theories	Publications, conference presentation and invited lectures/talks	Answering questions or feedback on his work

Value chain analysis is a detailed analysis of each activity of an organization on the criteria of the cost of the activity and value created by the activity, and reconfiguring the activities in a way that it creates competitive advantage for the organization.

Questions for you:

1. What is value chain analysis of your organization?

   ....

2. Is it good enough? If yes, why?

   ....

3. If not, how are you going to take care of it?

   ....
   ....
   ....

12. STRATEGIC ALTERNATIVES AND CHOICE

Let me show you a small video clip from the TBBT, season 5, episode 10.

At one point in this episode, Leonard and Sheldon are in their apartment. Leonard asks Sheldon if he can talk to him about something which is a little awkward. Sheldon jumps to his own conclusions without hearing Leonard out. He starts telling Leonard that he also agrees with Leonard that Leonard should abandon his research and focus on teaching. He goes further and suggests Leonard should change to an easier discipline such as history, where he has to just remember the past and tell it to students. Leonard stops him and tells him that Stuart is trying to date Amy and this is the actual awkward thing he wanted to talk about. Sheldon says he doesn't own Amy as slavery was abolished by President Lincoln in 1863 and Leonard should know these things if he wants to teach history.

Ha ha! This is hilarious.

In this video, Sheldon looks at the possible alternatives available to his roommate Leonard. According to Sheldon, Leonard as an experimental physicist is washed out. He suggests that Leonard should move to teaching, assuming it doesn't require much effort or intelligence. And then looking at the ease of just talking about the past and not creating anything new he recommends him to move to teaching history! What Sheldon is doing here is creating strategic alternatives and choosing one for Leonard for the rest of his life. Though Leonard doesn't agree with him.

Strategic alternatives mean an organization creates and evaluates various strategic options to achieve its stated vision and mission. And later chooses one strategy out of these alternatives.

Questions for you:

1. What are strategic alternatives and choice at your organization?

   ....
   ....
   ....

2. Are they good enough? If yes, why?

   ....
   ....
   ....

3. If not, how are you going to take care of it?

   ....
   ....
   ....

13. STRATEGY

Let me show you a small video clip from the TBBT, season 2, episode 2.

In this episode, Leslie and Leonard are in the apartment and Sheldon enters the apartment. He tells Leonard that he has no more objections to their relationship even though Leslie is an arrogant sub-par scientist. Then, Leslie and Sheldon argue about who is researching the better theory – Sheldon with string theory or Leslie with loop quantum theory. Sheldon believes in string theory whereas Leslie believes in loop quantum theory. They end up arguing a lot.

This is hilarious.

Sheldon's strategy from the beginning is to work in theoretical Physics and realize his vision of winning a Nobel Prize. During the whole series Sheldon sticks with physics and keeps trying to solve string theory or super-asymmetry. In-between he feels that physics is dead and considered alternatives but did not change his strategy. Later he and Amy achieved success in their attempts. Two physicists from Chicago, Dr. Campbell and Dr. Pemberton, accidentally prove Sheldon and Amy's super-asymmetry theory. This puts them on track for a Nobel Prize.

Strategy is choosing a unique position among the various alternatives possible and staying focused on that to achieve the desired vision.

Questions for you:

1. What is the strategy of your organization?

   ....
   ....
   ....

2. Is it good enough? If yes, why?

   ....
   ....
   ....

3. If not, how are you going to take care of it?

   ....
   ....
   ....

14. TACTICS

Let me show you a small video clip from the TBBT, season 5, episode 23.

In this episode, Sheldon goes to the apartment of Amy, where Amy suggests that they should progress in their relationship as all their other friends are doing the same. Sheldon wonders how much faster she wants to go as he is already in her house after dark whereas they did not even know each other two years ago! Then Amy plays the music from Super Mario Brothers, Sheldon's favourite childhood game, offers him a Strawberry Quik, a drink from his childhood and serves Spaghetti with the hot dog just like his mother used to make. Sheldon is overwhelmed by all this and suggests they do it more often!

This is hilarious. In this scene, Amy wants to move forward in her relationship with Sheldon. To do so, she uses tactics of offering Sheldon what he likes – music from childhood, his favourite drink i.e. strawberry Quik and his favourite food i.e. spaghetti with little pieces of hot dogs cut into it. Sheldon loves all this and ends up saying, we should do this more often, which Amy wants to do for sure!

Tactics are short terms activities for supporting and achieving the chosen strategy of an organization.

Questions for you:

1. What are the tactics for your organization?

   ....
   ....
   ....

2. Are they good enough? If yes, why?

   ....
   ....
   ....

3. If not, how are you going to take care of it?

   ....
   ....
   ....

15. COST LEADERSHIP STRATEGY

Let me show you a small video clip from the TBBT, season 6, episode 18.

In this episode, Leonard goes with Sheldon and Howard to a school to inspire young girls to pursue careers in science. All three try to inspire the girls in their own weird ways. Leonard ends up saying that he wanted to be a rap star but was forced to be a scientist by his parents who were also scientists! Sheldon ends the session by saying he hopes the little girls are discouraged by them from pursuing science.

This is hilarious. Leonard is putting some effort of time and energy into science but not all. He is also trying to be a bit social and achieve a work – life balance. He has seen his parents, mainly his mother, focusing too much on science, even treating him as the subject of experiments! As a teenager he wanted to be a rapper but was pushed into science by his parents. Thus he is not investing as much time or energy (his costs) as Sheldon in science and is happy with whatever he achieves (even lesser achievements) by doing so and not like Sheldon who is aiming towards a Noble prize for Physics.

To sustain against rivals in the industry, the concept of competitive strategy is used. There are two variables namely competitive scope and competitive advantage. There are three generic possibilities of low cost leadership, differentiation and focus. When your scope is wider and you are competing on low cost it is called cost leadership strategy. In this, the organization produces goods or services of comparable features at low cost compared to the competition in the industry.

Questions for you:

1. Is your organization following a cost leadership strategy?

   ....
   ....
   ....

2. Is it sustainable? If yes, why?

   ....
   ....
   ....

3. If not, how are you going to take care of it?

   ....
   ....
   ....

16. DIFFERENTIATION STRATEGY

Let me show you a small video clip from the TBBT, season 2, episode 6.

In this episode, Sheldon and Leonard are in a lecture room at the university. Leonard has finished his talk and invites Sheldon to tell present the theoretical physics department. Sheldon refuses to come out to talk because he thinks it is a waste of his time lecturing these average students. He finally agrees to do it when Leonard threatens to not take him to the comic book store. He rushes his presentation focusing on praising himself and making fun of the students. At the end when he asks whether the students have any questions, the students have no questions for him and he ends the session by saying he weeps for the future of science.

This is hilarious.

Sheldon is following a strategy of differentiation. He believes he has got great cognitive gifts and he needs to use those for science. He is investing a lot of time and energy in science to come up with a new theory to win a Nobel prize in Physics.

When your scope is wider and you are competing on creating something different or unique from others, it is differentiation strategy. In this, the organization spends resources to produce goods of unique features valued by customers who are willing to pay a higher price for that.

Questions for you:

1. Is your organization following a differentiation strategy?

   ....
   ....
   ....

2. Is it sustainable? If yes, why?

   ....
   ....
   ....

3. If not, how are you going to take care of it?

   ....
   ....
   ....

17. PLAN B

Let me share another fun video from TBBT, season 3, episode 9.

Sheldon is in his apartment kitchen with Leonard and Raj. He is preparing a solution of hydrogen peroxide and one of saturated potassium iodide to take revenge on Kripke. He puts large quantities of these chemicals above the tiles in the drop ceiling of Kripke's lab and sets a trap so a reaction will be triggered when Kripke reaches the center of the room. He watches the live shots of the lab on his laptop via a mini webcam. Unfortunately, Kirpke is accompanied by the president of the university and the board of directors. Sheldon has not planned any option to abort the revenge plan and when the group reaches the center of the room foam falls from the ceiling soaking everyone. To make it worse, a prerecorded message pops up on the laptop of Kripke in the lab in which Sheldon claims responsibility for the incident and also names Howard and Raj!

As seen in the video, Sheldon plans to take revenge on Kripke. Unfortunately, the president of the university walks in with Kirpky and he also becomes target of the planned trick of Sheldon. And Sheldon has no Plan B to abort or stop Plan A when it is known that it will go against him!

Plan B is keeping an alternative strategy ready, in case your main strategy i.e. Plan A doesn't work.

Questions for you:

1. Does your organization have a Plan B?

   ....
   ....
   ....

2. Is it good enough? If yes, why?

   ....
   ....
   ....

3. If not, how are you going to take care of it?

   ....
   ....
   ....

18. SCENARIO PLANNING

Here is another gem from TBBT, season 11, episode 12.

As you have seen, at one point in this episode, Sheldon and Amy are in her apartment. Amy is worried about how they are going to choose a maid of honour and best men for the wedding without hurting the emotions of their friends. Sheldon suggests they make the decision based on data and keep emotions out of it. Amy likes this as they can choose but they are not responsible for hurting the feelings of their friends because data is going to be responsible for the decision. Sheldon suggests people perform very specific functions in marriage and not all are going to be good. Amy agrees with this and suggests they break down every role into parts and develop a specialized test for their friends for each part. Sheldon ends up saying that if knew getting married will involve so much science, he would have proposed much earlier!

It is so much fun! In this video, Sheldon and Amy are trying to choose the best man and maid of honour for their wedding respectively. They deduce that these roles require you to fulfil certain responsibilities. They want to ensure that the person who can manage all circumstances most efficiently will be chosen for the roles. For this they create certain circumstances intentionally and score their friends on their performance. Here we can see Sheldon and Amy creating alternate possibilities of expected wedding emergencies and finding the best person who can tackle them.

Organizations make assumptions and forecasts, and based on that create alternate possibilities for future called scenarios, and creating contingency plans is called scenario planning.

Questions for you:

1. Does your organization use scenario planning?

   ....
   ....
   ....

2. Is it good enough? If yes, why?

   ....
   ....
   ....

3. If not, how are you going to take care of it?

   ....
   ....
   ....

19. DIVERSIFICATION (ANSOFF MATRIX)

Let me show you a funny video clip from the TBBT, season 3, episode 10.

In this episode, Sheldon is in the apartment and Penny joins him. She asks him to teach her some physics. She requests that he teach her just enough so she can talk to Leonard about his job. Sheldon asks her to learn from Leonard but she refuses to do so because she wants to surprise Leonard and this is important to her. Sheldon tries to teach her physics from the beginning which Penny finds very difficult. Finally, Sheldon teaches her what Leonard does and she is happy about it. Later, she surprises Leonard with her knowledge about his work.

In this scene Penny request Sheldon to teach her a little Physics so that she can understand what Leonard does. So in this Penny is going to diversify her knowledge by learning some Physics for the existing boyfriend, Leonard.

New Markets	Penny with a new guy with same knowledge	Penny with a new guy with knowledge of physics
Existing Markets	Penny with Leonard with same knowledge	Penny with Leonard with knowledge of physics
	Existing Products	New Products

Diversification is one way of growth for an organization when it goes into newer businesses which may or may not relate to its current business. Ansoff Matrix gives the various ways in which a company can expand its business. For existing markets or new markets and existing products or new products, it creates four possibilities of market penetration, market expansion, product expansion and diversification.

Questions for you:

1. What is diversification at your organization?

   ....
   ....
   ....

2. Is it good enough? If yes, why?

   ....
   ....
   ....

3. If not, how are you going to take care of it?

   ....
   ....
   ....

20. STRATEGIC ALLIANCES

Let me show you this hilarious video from TBBT season 4, episode 18.

At one point in this episode, in the university cafeteria, Sheldon is with Raj and Howard. Howard is performing some magic trick involving cards on Raj. Sheldon asks him not to waste time on these silly things. Howard challenges Sheldon to figure out how the trick works. Sheldon tries to figure out the trick for days but fails. Howard mocks him and tries to perform the trick again on Raj. Sheldon asks him to perform the trick on him as he suspects some monkey business. In fact, there is an understanding between Raj and Howard and Raj tips Howard about the details of the card taken by Sheldon. Sheldon is outsmarted again in the magic trick by Howard and Raj.

This is hilarious! Ha ha!

On a serious note, as you see in this video, Howard and Raj form an alliance to outsmart Sheldon in a magic trick of cards.

Sheldon thinks he can outsmart them but the alliance of Raj and Howard outsmarts Sheldon in the magic trick.

Strategic alliance is the coming together of two or more organizations for mutual gain. When these two organizations form a separate legal entity then that kind of alliance is called a joint venture.

Questions for you:

1. Does your organization use strategic alliances?

   ....
   ....
   ....

2. Are they working well for your organization? If yes, why?

   ....
   ....
   ....

3. If not, how are you going to take care of it?

   ....
   ....
   ....

21. CO-OPETITION

Let me share this hilarious video from TBBT season 12, episode 13.

As you have seen, at one point in this episode, in the university restaurant, Sheldon and Amy are introduced to two other scientist Dr. Campbell and Dr. Pemberton. Sheldon and Amy have come up with a theory on super-asymmetry which was accidentally proven by Dr. Campbell and Dr. Pemberton. Their theory is groundbreaking and could be in line for a Nobel prize. All four want to be in the running for the Nobel prize for physics but a shared Nobel prize can only be awarded to a maximum of three people. Dr. Campbell and Dr. Pemberton suggest to Sheldon that they need to drop Amy's name from the application for the Nobel prize for physics. Sheldon doesn't like it and feels they are stealing the Nobel prize from Amy and him. Later, he is made to understand that their chances of being awarded the Nobel prize are best if both their institutions recommend three names only, excluding Amy. Finally, unwillingly, he agrees to this.

Ha ha! It is great!

Coming back to strategy, in this, Sheldon and Amy come

up with the concept of 'Super Asymmetry' but Dr. Campbell and Dr. Pemberton prove it with experiments, though by accident. Both the teams are competing for the chance to get a Nobel Prize for the work but their chances are greater if they go together and they decide to go together. This is co-opetition.

Co-opetition is the strategy of competing as well as co-operating with your competition on certain things for mutual gains.

Questions for you:

1. What is the co-opetition for your organization?

   ....
   ....
   ....

2. Is it working well for your organization? If yes, why?

   ....
   ....
   ....

3. If not, how are you going to take care of it?

   ....
   ....
   ....

22. BUSINESS MODEL

Let me share another hilarious video from TBBT season 5, episode 12.

In this episode, the scene is a birthday party where Howard is performing as a magician and Bernadette is playing the role of his assistant. Howard is performing magic tricks for the kids. One kid asks for the cake and Bernadette tells him to wait till the end of the performance. The kid asks again after some time and Bernadette loses her cool a bit. She gets distracted and gives a real pitcher full of milk to Howard for a trick that is supposed to use a fake pitcher of milk. The front side of Howard gets all wet as his trick fails.

Ha ha! It is so funny. From a strategy perspective, this is a good one to understand the concept of a business model canvas. The business model canvas for Howard is as follows.

Key Partners	Key Activities	Value Proposition	Customer Relationship Management	Customer Segment
Suppliers of equipment's, costumers and food used in the show.	Performing magic tricks, jokes as fillers, arranging the settings for magic show.	Only value proposition is cake and food (Because tricks were old and performed badly).	Bad customer relationship management as Bernadette is very poor in dealing with kids	Kids who might like magic tricks
	Key Resources Magic tricks, Bernadette as assistant, and costumes & settings.		**Delivery** Live performance.	
Cost Costs of materials used. Time and efforts of the host.		**Revenue** Satisfaction from entertaining the kids. Helping Bernadette to learn dealing with kids.		

A business model is the way an organization identifies target customers, creates value for them and makes some profit out of this. A detailed concept is a business model canvas which consists of nine blocks as discussed for Howard.

Questions for you:

1. What is the business model canvas of your organization?

   ....
   ....
   ....

2. Is it good enough? If yes, why?

   ....
   ....
   ....

3. If not, how are you going to take care of it?

   ....
   ....
   ....

23. STRATEGY EXECUTION

Here is another funny video from TBBT, season 11, episode 12.

In one scene in this episode, Amy and Sheldon are driving to Howard's apartment. Amy asks Sheldon to do her a favour and change the topic of conversation if the topic of their wedding comes up. She says so because she doesn't want to discuss who is going to be her maid of honour as she has not decided it yet and she wants to avoid being caught in a difficult situation between Penny and Bernadette. Sheldon agrees to this and they decide whenever Amy says the code word pretzel, Sheldon will change the topic of the conversation away from the wedding. They reach Howard's Apartment. After some time, Howard brings up the topic of their wedding and Amy uses the code word pretzel. Sheldon tries to change the topic but he ends up talking about the food at their wedding!

From the video we can see Amy is confused about picking her maid of honor for wedding, and asks Sheldon to help her change the subject whenever the subject of "wedding" comes up. As usual Sheldon suggests an idea - The use of a code word! Amy told Sheldon to strategically change the subject when the code word 'Pretzel' is used so that the maid of honor topic is not brought into picture. In the scene, Howard brings up the topic, Sheldon deviates upon hearing the word "pretzel". Unfortunately, he fails to execute the strategy as he comes up with a story of pretzel at a wedding.

Strategy execution is the process of implementing the chosen strategy, to reach the desired vision. Strategy execution is where the real fun in strategy beings. There are some problems an organizations faces while implementing a strategy and these are called execution troubles.

Questions for you:

1. How is strategy execution at your organization?

   ....
   ....
   ....

2. Is it good enough? If yes, why?

   ....
   ....
   ....

3. If not, how are you going to take care of it?

   ....
   ....
   ....

24. RESOURCE ALLOCATION

Here you go with another fun video from TBBT season 9, episode 3.

As you have seen, at one point in this episode, the scene is the four friends in a van in Mexico. Suddenly they find out one of the tyres is flat. They try to change the flat tyre but find it difficult. They challenge themselves to solve this problem as it is just a physics problem. They try different methods using the available resources and end up burning the van.

Ha ha! This is hilarious.

In this episode, Sheldon and his friends got into a situation where they had a flat tire. They could not fix it because they were using the wrong equipment and methods. Finally, by using the wrong resources, they managed to burn their car!

Choosing a strategy in itself is of no use if proper resource allocation is not done to support the chosen strategy.

Questions for you:

1. How is the resource allocation at your organization?

   ....
   ....
   ....

2. Is it good enough? If yes, why?

   ....
   ....
   ....

3. If not, how are you going to take care of it?

   ....
   ....
   ....

25. GROWTH TRAP

Let me share another hilarious video with you from TBBT, season 6, episode 12.

In this episode, Leonard runs into Penny in the stairwell of their building. Penny asks Leonard why he looks extra happy. Leonard gives some explanation about his workday going well, winning some Star Trek quiz online, and more so getting to spend time with Penny. Penny is not amused and questions him about his liking of Alex, Sheldon's assistant, hitting on him. Penny doesn't like him enjoying the attention of another woman.

Ha ha. It is hilarious. In this video, Leonard seems extra happy to Penny, and Penny asks him about it. Leonard says a couple of things avoiding revealing the real reason for his happiness. Penny gets irritated by this and asks him to go spend the evening with another girl who is hitting on him. This is a classic example of growth trap that organizations fall into. Instead of enjoying and staying focused on one successful relationship, Leonard is mindlessly enjoying being hit by another woman and risking his relationship with Penny.

Even after choosing a strategy, organizations are lured into mindless growth for which they deviate from the chosen strategy and that creates trouble.

Questions for you:

1. Does your organization avoid growth traps?

   ....
   ....
   ....

2. Is it successful in doing so? If yes, why?

   ....
   ....
   ....

3. If not, how are you going to take care of it?

   ....
   ....
   ....

26. FOCUS & DISCIPLINE

You need to watch this from TBBT, season 5, episode 18.

As you have seen, at one point in this episode, the scene is in Bernadette's bedroom. Bernadette is talking to Howard on Skype. Howard is going through survival training in the wilderness with NASA in preparation for his upcoming mission to the International Space Station. He looks exhausted and battered. Bernadette is worried and asks what is happening to him. He tells her that with his bare hands he dug a hole in the ground to sleep and an armadillo crawled into it and spooned him, he survived a sandstorm and ate a butterfly. He found his inner strength to keep going and will complete the training to realize his dream of going to space.

Ha ha! It is hilarious!

In this video, Howard is undergoing survival training for NASA. This training is very tough for him as he shares his experiences of digging a hole for with his bare hands to make a place for sleeping, and ended up eating a butterfly because he was so hungry! He stayed focused and disciplined to complete it, because he wants to fulfill his strategy of being an astronaut!

Focus and discipline suggest that once the organization has chosen a particular strategy, it needs to stay focused and disciplined on implementing it.

Questions for you:

1. Does your organization stays focused and disciplined for the chosen strategy?

   ....
   ....
   ....

2. Is it successful in doing so? If yes, why?

   ....
   ....
   ....

3. If not, how are you going to take care of it?

   ....
   ....
   ....

27. CURSE OF KNOWLEDGE

Let me share another funny video from TBBT, season 11, episode 13.

As you have seen, at one point in this episode, the scene is Sheldon's apartment. Sheldon is talking about physics to Penny while she is appreciating the pizza they are eating. He keeps talking about his love for string theory and its importance and that even Einstein couldn't figure it out. Penny suggests him it might be just wrong if even Einstein could not figure it out. That doesn't stop Sheldon and he keeps talking about string theory.

This is hilarious.

This conversation between Sheldon Cooper and Penny is a classic example of the curse of knowledge. He forgets/assumes that Penny has no background in Physics and begins without giving necessary context and facts, and Penny is seen to be clueless.

The curse of knowledge is assuming everyone is at the same level of understanding or knowledge as you are and then not explaining things in details and properly.

Questions for you:

1. Does your organization avoid curse of knowledge?

   ....
   ....
   ....

2. Is it successful in doing so? If yes, why?

   ....
   ....
   ....

3. If not, how are you going to take care of it?

   ....
   ....
   ....

28. IMPORTANCE OF ASSUMPTIONS

Here is another one from TBBT season 2, episode 11.

As you have seen, at one point in this episode, the scene is Sheldon's apartment. Sheldon tells Leonard that he has solved his Penny gift dilemma as he has brought a number of gifts of different prices and will exchange the gift closest to the cost of the gift given by Penny and return the rest of the gifts. Penny then enters with a gift for Leonard and a napkin used by Leonard Nimoy for Sheldon. Sheldon is a huge fan of Leonard Nimoy. Sheldon is overwhelmed by his gift as it is priceless to him and so gives all the gifts he has bought to Penny and even hugs her!

This is hilarious. In this video, Sheldon assumes Penny is going to buy some gift from the market for him for Christmas, and he can give her a gift of similar price. As he doesn't know how much she will spend, Sheldon buys multiple gifts in different price ranges so he can give Penney a gift that matches what she spent on him. To his surprise, Penny gives him something which is not from market and thus has no price. On top of it, the gift is priceless for Sheldon and he gives all the gifts he brought plus a hug to penny.

For the success of any strategy, making the right assumptions on which the strategy is based is very important. If assumptions are wrong, the strategy will fail.

Questions for you:

1. What are the major assumptions behind strategy of your organization?

   ....
   ....
   ....

2. Are these good enough? If yes, why?

   ....
   ....
   ....

3. If not, how are you going to take care of it?

   ....
   ....
   ....

29. PARALYSIS BY ANALYSIS

Here is a real fun video for you from TBBT season 7, episode 19.

In this episode, Sheldon and Amy are in an electrical store. Sheldon has come to buy a new games console. He has narrowed down his choices to either a PS4 or an Xbox. He has done a lot of research on these two consoles including an informal poll before coming to the store. The previous night over dinner he had driven Amy crazy comparing the pros and cons of PS4 and Xbox, getting so distracted he even forget to pass salt as requested by Amy. In the store, he keeps comparing the two for a long time, Amy falls asleep as it is taking him so long. Later they are asked to leave the store by the store assistant as it is time to close the store. Sheldon insists on staying as he has not decided which console to buy but he is told they need to leave.

In this video, Sheldon is analyzing two game consoles namely Xbox vs PS4. He goes crazy about it by going into too much analysis while having dinner with Amy. They go to the shop and there Sheldon takes a lot of time in analyzing the consoles, so much so that the shop is closed and they are asked to leave without a games console.

Paralysis by analysis means some analysis is required but it is more important to take a decision and act otherwise you would be still analyzing and someone else will run away with the customers!

Questions for you:

1. Does your organization faces paralysis by analysis situations?

   ....
   ....
   ....

2. What is your organization doing to avoid these situations?

   ....
   ....
   ....

3. How your organization can ensure that it doesn't suffer from paralysis by analysis?

   ....
   ....
   ....

30. STRATEGIC ALIGNMENT

Here is another hilarious one from TBBT, season 2, episode 6.

As you have seen, at one point in this episode, the scene is Sheldon's apartment. Sheldon is working while Ramona is taking care of him. Leonard enters the apartment and reminds Sheldon it is Wednesday and Wednesday is Halo night. Sheldon agrees and wants to go with him. He is stopped by Ramona who reminds him what he has said earlier about the unconditional dedication of their entire lives for science. Sheldon agrees with her and tells Leonard he can't argue with himself. Leonard lives the apartment a bit frustrated and Sheldon goes back to work.

Ha ha! I love it.

In this video, Sheldon is reminded again and again of his strategy of focusing on science and his vision to win a Nobel Prize for Physics. He is reminded again and again that all his actions should be aligned towards achieving the vision with the strategy to focus on science. But the way it is done is so hilarious!

Strategic alignment means that all activities of an organization should be aligned with the chosen strategy of the organisation.

Questions for you:

1. How is strategic alignment at your organization?

   ....
   ....
   ....

2. Is it good enough? If yes, why?

   ....
   ....
   ....

3. If not, how are you going to take care of it?

   ....
   ....
   ....

31. ENTREPRENEURSHIP

Here is a funny video for you from TBBT season 2, episode 18.

In this episode, Sheldon and Penny are in Penny's apartment. Penny tells Sheldon that she has started a new business making flower Barrettes which she calls Penny Blossoms. She discovered this business opportunity accidentally and if it works she thinks she will not need to work as a waitress anymore. Sheldon asks her questions about her business model, does some calculations and tells her that based on her current business model she will make a profit of USD 2600 in a year. Penny asks Sheldon to help her in making more money with this business to which Sheldon agrees.

Ha ha! It is so funny.
In this video, Penny starts a new business of Penny Blossoms.
And as with many entrepreneurs, she has no idea about the profit she will make and other aspects of business.
Sheldon agrees to help her in this.

Entrepreneurship is about creating new ventures.

Questions for you:

1. How is entrepreneurship at your organization?

   ....
   ....
   ....

2. Is it good enough? If yes, why?

   ....
   ....
   ....

3. If not, how are you going to take care of it?

   ....
   ....
   ....

32. INNOVATION

Here is another gem from TBBT for you from season 3, episode 14.

As you have seen, at one point in this episode, the scene is the Cheesecake Factory restaurant. To the surprise of Penny, Sheldon just walks in and starts working there without getting hired. Later Sheldon drops a tray and Sheldon is dumbstruck. He observes the broken tray pieces on the ground and identifies the interference pattern in the fracture and realizes that electrons move through the graphene as a wave and not particles! He leaves the place even without cleaning the mess he has created as he doesn't work there!

Ha ha! This is so good.

In this video, Sheldon is working for free in this restaurant. He drops the plates by mistakes. Suddenly, while looking at the broken plates on the ground, he gets an innovative idea by combining broken plates with the movement of electrons! This is something similar to the famous graduation speech 'connecting the dots' by Steve Jobs at Stanford University.

Innovation is something new which creates commercial or social value or both.

Questions for you:

1. How is innovation at your organization?

   ....
   ....
   ....

2. Is it good enough? If yes, why?

   ....
   ....
   ....

3. If not, how are you going to take care of it?

   ....
   ....
   ....

33. INTERNATIONAL STRATEGY

Here you go with another gem from TBBT, season 1, episode 8.

In this scene, set in the Cheesecake Factory, Penny is serving at the bar. Leonard, Howard, and Sheldon are introduced by Raj to his Indian date Lalita Gupta. Sheldon finds her face similar to an Indian Princess Punchali, a beloved character from an Indian folk tale. He praises her which makes Raj uncomfortable as he thinks Sheldon is hitting on his date. He asks Sheldon to stay away from her but she tells him to shut up and asks Sheldon to talk more about that Indian princess. She asks Sheldon out for dinner and they leave the group to the surprise of everyone!

Ha ha! This is so much fun.

As we see in this video, Sheldon uses his knowledge about an Indian character from one of the comic books he has read as a kid to interact with the Indian girl who came to meet his friend Raj. And incidentally, she ended up inviting Sheldon for food and ditching Raj.

International strategy is the strategy of an organization involved in business in more than one country for dealing with international business.

Questions for you:

1. How is international strategy at your organization?

   ....
   ....
   ....

2. Is it good enough? If yes, why?

   ....
   ....
   ....

3. If not, how are you going to take care of it?

   ....
   ....
   ....

34. CORPORATE GOVERNANCE

I must share this fantastic video from TBBT, season 6, episode 20.

As you have seen, at one point in this episode, the scene is the university gymnasium. Leonard goes there and starts talking to Mrs. Davis and starts using the treadmill. He needs Mrs. Davis' help to use the treadmill as he is not familiar with them. He talks about his candidature for tenure as she is on the committee who will decide who gets tenure. Later in the day, Mrs. Davis receives a self-promotional video from Raj and a personal visit from Sheldon. All of them are candidates for the tenure position and Mrs. Davis is one of the committee members and each one tries to impress her in weird ways.

Isn't it hilarious? This scene shows how the friends fight immorally for a tenure position. They try to persuade the panel by using unfair means and not keeping it strictly professional. We see Leonard joining the same gym as one of the panel member, Raj makes a special video about himself for her and Sheldon gives her a gift. All these portray how they try to get an edge over others to get the tenure position.

Corporate governance refers to how the organization is governed and run. The most important components are transparency, accountability and fairness.

Questions for you:

1. How is corporate governance at your organization?

   ....
   ....
   ....

2. Is it good enough? If yes, why?

   ....
   ....
   ....

3. If not, how are you going to take care of it?

   ....
   ....
   ....

35. STRATEGIC CORPORATE SOCIAL RESPONSIBILITY (CSR)

Here is another fun video from TBBT, season 4, episode 14.

As you have seen, at one point in this episode, Sheldon is in a lecture hall. He delivers a session just praising himself and making fun of the doctoral students. The students are bored in the lecture and they start posting nasty tweets about the lecture. These tweets are read by Howard, Leonard, and Raj who is back in the apartment and Penny also joins them. When Sheldon goes back to the apartment he claims his lecture was triumphant. He sees the others reading tweets and read the tweets on his lecture. He finds the tweets quite unfair and claims he didn't want to teach those poopy heads anyway.

Ha ha! It is hilarious!

In this video, Sheldon goes to a class to share his knowledge with PhD students. From his perspective, he was taking time out of his busy research work as he felt it was his duty to share what he knows with the brightest students of the university. From his perspective he was doing strategic CSR by sharing his knowledge with students and having fun with the brightest students. However, it turned out to be a nightmare for him!

Strategic CSR is not philanthropy. Strategic CSR is done in such a way that it helps the organization as well as the receiver of it.

Questions for you:

1. How is strategic CSR managed at your organization?
   ....
   ....
   ....

2. Is it good enough? If yes, why?
   ....
   ....
   ....

3. If not, how are you going to take care of it?
   ....
   ....
   ....

36. ORGANIZATIONAL STRUCTURE

Get ready to watch another hilarious video from TBBT, season 4, episode 12.

As you have seen, at one point in this episode, the four friends are in Sheldon's apartment. Sheldon shares a workflow chart with a list of duties and designations for developing an app based on an idea Leonard had. Leonard doesn't like that Sheldon is taking over and says he should be in charge of this project as it is his idea. Sheldon agrees and says that's why he has given Leonard the title of Founder in the organizational chart. Leonard points out that Sheldon is listed as Chief Executive Officer, Chief Financial Officer, and Chief Operating Officer. Sheldon adds that Leonard has missed Chief Science Officer, Chairman of the Board, and Head of the Secret Santa Committee which is also designations Sheldon has assigned himself.

Ha ha!

In this scene, Sheldon and his friends are working on the development of an app, the idea of which was conceived by Leonard. In order to do the work, Sheldon assigns roles and responsibilities to everyone as follows:

Rajesh: Phone Support
Howard: Executive Assistant
Leonard: Founder

Sheldon: CFO, COO, CEO, Chief Science Officer, Chairman of the Board, Head of Secret Santa Committee.

Each member has specific duties to perform under the leadership and guidance of their (supposed) leader, Sheldon, for the development of the app.

The various activities in an organization are arranged into departments and the whole organization is arranged in a hierarchy with roles and responsibilities. This is called a structure.

Questions for you:

1. What is your organizational structure?

   ....
   ....
   ....

2. Is it good enough? If yes, why?

   ....
   ....
   ....

3. If not, how are you going to take care of it?

   ....
   ....
   ....

37. MCKINSEY 7S FRAMEWORK

Here is another hilarious gem from TBBT for you from season 8, episode 12.

As you have seen, at one point in this episode, the scene is in a clothes shop. Amy and Penny are shopping while Sheldon and Leonard are waiting for them. Sheldon gets upset about the fact that Leonard will be moving out of their apartment to move in with Penny. Sheldon accepts that he is a difficult person to live with and thanks Leonard for putting up with him. They are joined by Amy and Penny. Penny tells Sheldon that Leonard is not going to move out completely till he is ready. Sheldon suggests that Leonard's move should happen gradually. This leads to Sheldon and Leonard negotiating on the details of the moving out of Leonard.

On a serious note, here is Mckinsey 7S framework for roommates Sheldon and Leonard.

7S Component	For Sheldon & Leonard
Strategy	To live together with another geek with common interests and the same workplace.
Structure	Autocratic structure where Sheldon dominates.
Systems	Detailed routines in place according to the roommate agreement.
Super ordinate Goals	Scientific discoveries and geek time together.
Skills	Soft skills (not much) and hard skills (analysis, scientific knowledge).
Staff	No direct staff. Friends act as support.
Style	Participatory but dominated by Sheldon

Mckinsey 7S is a framework to access and ensure that strategy, structure, systems, super ordinate goals, skills, staff and style of organization fit together in a mutually supportive way for good performance.

Questions for you:

1. What is McKinsey 7S framework for your organization?

   ....

2. Is it good enough? If yes, why?

   ....

3. If not, how are you going to take care of it?

   ....
   ....
   ....

38. EMERGENT STRATEGY

Here is a hilarious one from TBBT for you from session 5, episode 18.

As you have seen, at one point in this episode, the scene is Sheldon's apartment. Penny and Leonard are inside the apartment and Sheldon walk in. Penny is sitting on Sheldon's spot and offers to vacate it for Sheldon. To their surprise, Sheldon doesn't want it. He says he has spent his entire life carefully planning everything but recently made some changes and nothing horrible has happened to him. He is six days late for his haircut and it had not brought him misfortune. He laments that he was unnecessary in planning all his life in detail. To comfort him, Penny says it is nice not knowing what is coming and gives the example of her relationship with Leonard. Sheldon sees her point.

Haha!

In this video, Sheldon is upset that nothing bad has happened to him even when he is six days past his hair cut. He feels there is no point in planning everything. Penny chips in by saying that it is better to just go with life and see what happens. This is somewhat similar to emergent strategy rather than the hierarchy approach to strategy.

The idea that an organization looks back and identifies how its strategy has emerged over a period of time is called emergent strategy. It is opposite of the thought that the firm always starts with a well-defined strategy and sticks to it.

Questions for you:

1. What is the emergent strategy for your organization?

   ....
   ....
   ....

2. Is it good enough? If yes, why?

   ....
   ....
   ....

3. If not, how are you going to take care of it?

   ....
   ....
   ....

39. BALANCED SCORECARD

I am sure you will love this. Here is another funny one for you from TBBT, season 10, episode 14.

As you have seen, at one point in this episode, the scene is Raj's apartment. Raj is with Howard and he has invited his ex-girlfriends to learn from them why did they break up with him. Lucy says he kept trying to force her into uncomfortable situations. Claire says she broke up with him because he was really needy. When the conversation starts getting really heated, Raj suggests ending the discussion. In the end, all the girls say they found a better man after breaking up with Raj. Howard also jokes that he also found Bernadette after going out with Raj!

In this video, Raj has invited his ex-girlfriends to give feedback on him. It is interesting to evaluate his performance using a Balanced Scorecard.

Financial Perspective: He is still single, so he is not performing well here. (It measures financial data i.e. numbers. In this case it is zero in terms of his girlfriends)

Customer Perspective: All the ex-girlfriends are saying negative things about him. This is not a good performance.

Internal Process Perspective: He has not put any deliberate processes in place to be better at relationships with girls. He only has one process i.e. to get drunk so that he can talk to girls.

Learning & Growth Perspective: His behavior in the video shows he is not learning anything, even now from the good feedback he is getting.

Balanced Scorecard is a comprehensive tool to evaluate performance. It consists of four parts namely financial perspective, customer perspective, internal process perspective and learning & growth perspective.

Questions for you:

1. What is the Balanced Scorecard for your organization?

   ....
   ....
   ....

2. Is it good enough? If yes, why?

   ....
   ....
   ....

3. If not, how are you going to take care of it?

   ....
   ....
   ....

40. LIMITATIONS OF STRATEGY

Here is another good one from TBBT, season 4, episode 5.

As you have seen, at one point in this episode, the scene is Sheldon's apartment. Sheldon is panicked by Amy's suggestion of meeting her mother. He tells Leonard he is removing all digital footprints and also changes the nameplate of their apartment so that Amy cannot find him. He has sent a relationship termination notice to Amy and changed his mobile number and email address. However, Amy comes and knocks at the door of the apartment as she has been there a number of times. Sheldon is surprised at the failure of his perfect plan.

It is hilarious! Ha ha!

In this video, Sheldon makes a strategy to avoid meeting Amy and for that he changes his address (without changing the actual place), email and phone number. Obviously Amy finds his residence easily! Many organizations make strategies like this and it's no secret why so many of these strategies fail!

As in life, so in strategy, there is no guarantee of success. Strategy has its limitations and there is a need for both analysis and intuition in strategy.

Questions for you:

1. How does your organisation take care of the limitations of strategy?

   ....
   ....
   ....

2. Is it good enough? If yes, why?

   ....
   ....
   ....

3. If not, how are you going to take care of it?

   ....
   ....
   ....

THE LANDING ANNOUNCEMENT

There is an announcement about the plane approaching the destination.
Kapil: It was great!
Pushkar: Amazing! I never thought that strategy can be so much fun!
Professor: Yes, it is fun!
Kapil: Thank you so much. I am never going to forget any of these concepts now.
Pushkar: Me too! Thank you Professor.
Professor: You are welcome.
And they prepare for landing.

REFERENCES

The strategy concepts explained in the book are given by number of professors and some practitioners and these are available in any standard strategy book such as:

Hitt, M. A., Ireland, R. D., & Hoskisson, R. E. (2012). *Strategic management cases: competitiveness and globalization.* Cengage Learning.

Osterwalder, A., & Pigneur, Y. (2010). *Business model generation: a handbook for visionaries, game changers, and challengers.* John Wiley & Sons.

I have provided the series and episode reference for each video referenced in this book. You can watch the full episodes available on various platforms such as Amazon, CBS etc.

The brief explanation of some of the concepts are taken from my earlier books Love Strategy and Happiness Strategy.

APPENDIX 1.
FREE RESOURCES FOR STRATEGY

1. Free membership websites for latest articles on strategy.

   http://knowledge.wharton.upenn.edu/
   https://sloanreview.mit.edu/
   https://cmr.berkeley.edu/blog/
   https://hbr.org/topic/strategy
   https://www.mckinsey.com/quarterly/
   https://www.bcgperspectives.com/

2. There are free videos on YouTube by leading thinkers in strategy. You can easily find it through google search. E.g.

   https://www.youtube.com/user/HarvardBSchool/videos

3. There are number of courses on strategy available for free on MIT OpenCourseWare and similar platforms. You can easily find it through google search. E.g. https://ocw.mit.edu/index.htm

4. For a humorous perspective on strategy and innovation, visit www.pillania.org and watch YouTube channel of Prof. Rajesh Pillania

BRIEF PROFILE OF THE AUTHOR

Dr. Rajesh K Pillania is rated and awarded the Top Professor of Strategy in India by ASSOCHAM and Education Post. He is ranked jointly number one in average research productivity among management faculty (including IIMs/IITs) in India for research output from 1968 to 2014 [By Prof Ramdhar Singh of IIM Banglore and others in 2015 which was published in a reputed international journal titled Omega in 2017]. He is on the advisory board of many esteemed international research journals, professional bodies and conferences consisting of leading international academicians, industry leaders and policy makers.

He is passionate about strategy and his areas of expertise are strategy, innovation strategy, strategy in India, global strategy, demystifying strategy, strategic humour and happiness strategy. His research is focused on two broad areas. First one is on the frontiers of strategic management and second one is on democratizing strategy. For frontiers of strategic management, he is involved with a number of esteemed international research journals and has written research papers and books. For democratizing strategy, he has published innovative humourous books which are available on Amazon, offers strategy workshops, and writes on strategy in popular media such as Times of India and The Economic Times, etc.

Besides being a prolific writer and a popular teacher; he has conducted various executive development programs for middle to senior management and, has conducted consulting assignments for top management of organizations. He is Professor of Strategy with MDI Gurgaon and holds a Ph.D in Strategy. His academic and research experience includes University Business School, Panjab University (Chandigarh, India); Management Development Institute (Gurgaon, India); Indian Institute of Management Kozhikode (Kozhikode, India); R. H. Smith School of Business, University of Maryland (Maryland, USA); Harvard University (Boston, USA); and MCI Management Centre (Innsbruck, Austria) among others. For more, please visit www.pillania.org and he can be reached at rajesh@pillania.org

EXECUTIVE DEVELOPMENT PROGRAMS/TRAINING

Some of the training programs offered by Prof Rajesh Pillania are given below.

1. Strategic Humour: Strategy Made Easy for All
2. Innovation Humour: Innovation Made Easy for All.
3. Strategy for High Performance
4. Innovations for High Performance
5. Strategy with Intuition
6. Disruptive Strategy
7. Happiness Strategy
8. Humour for All
9. Key MBA Learnings for All.

For more, please visit www.pillania.org and he can be reached at rajesh@pillania.org

www.ingramcontent.com/pod-product-compliance
Lightning Source LLC
Chambersburg PA
CBHW070438180526
45158CB00019B/1653